OMENS

Other books by Solee MacIsaac

Joy Shared

A Beloved Speck in the Universe

Little Wisdoms

Zen Days, Zen Nights

Harvest

Songs of Immortality

Soul Blossoms

Amuse-Bouches

Omens

Solee MacIsaac

EVERY BOOK PRESS

MMXXVI

Book Design:
William Bentley

INTRODUCTION

Omens is a collection of thoughts written from April through August 2024, mostly in conjunction with *Amuse-Bouches*. It is meant to suggest an entrance into objective reality. If successful, some thoughts may be difficult to ingest. All are meant in good humor and love for all readers.

Solee MacIsaac

Omens *is dedicated to everyone who has befriended me in the space of my life. All of you have influenced me and shown me the way to proceed, even when I didn't recognize it at the time. Thank you.*

Omens foretell
Events of import,
When ready to be received.

OMENS

Extreme intervention
Happens to realign
Levels.

A stemmed wine glass
Shattered in the sink today,
New person saw with my eyes.

With age – lines appear,
Frowns threaten permanency;
   In the Earth – cracks open.

Leaving behind old attitudes,
Accepting things as they are:
   A thin line of Light appears.

Once splintering begins,
Cracks race
   In all directions.

Windows rattling,
Wind flinging branches,
   Fierce storm rumbles on.

A shocking change,
Disturbing stasis,
   Enables new perspectives.

Tears come unbidden
When powerful beauty
   Embraces one's heart.

Kittens have soft fur,
Beautiful eyes,
And sharp claws.

When cracks appear
Be certain right things escape,
And right things enter.

Pervasive unshadowed light
Clears debris,
Defines all in supreme clarity.

Not much fits
Through the needle's eye,
Except our own Eye.

Driving over bumps in the road
Can shock the senses,
But impractical to stay awake.

The fine vibration of light
Is enough to sustain
Highly charged invisible beings.

Intensity of Light
Will leak through
Even tiny cracks.

For something
To shatter,
First cracks appear.

Love is too strong
Not to break
Old bonds.

Splinters, shards
Of light,
    Pierce to the center of being.

Happy tales
Are for the young,
    Truth demands reality.

Love nurtures,
Love sustains,
    Love breaks open.

Friction is useful
And can feel harsh,
    Until results are understood.

Myself as I am.
But what will
    I be?

Six keys
Open the doorway
    Wider and wider.

Don't hold back,
Loving all the way
Is essential.

Lightning cracks,
Shocking eyes and ears
With dangerous vibrations.

The body garment
Is quickly cast aside,
When we are free to fly.

A rock cairn rests
On shady ground;
    Reminder of lost love.

Deepening twilight
Sinks into shadows
    Beyond the back door.

An owl shrieks
In the night,
    Heavy wings flapping.

Shivering omens
Crawl along the ground,
    Disturbing longed for rest.

Predictions are not for
Tomorrow,
    Everything grows from now.

Watching for signs
Is an interesting prospect,
    But who is watching?

Symbols educate
Higher mind,
	Through silent images.

To be out of your mind
Is better
	Than to be in it.

Impossible to calculate
All the factors
	That create our lives.

Seen from above
It is obvious,
    All is as it must be.

We are given a lot,
Yet we struggle,
    Always climbing sunward.

Like flypaper
We are stuck
    To ourselves.

Why do we have words like
Infinite, eternal, forever?
Hints from above.

Love moves through
Dimensions
Without barriers.

Lost items
Sometimes find their way
Home.

Grief cannot be measured,
Lessened, or remedied;
But is lived through eventually.

When something is
'Life or Death,'
Choose life.

Even the dark parts
Of Earth
Have their own light.

Embers nestled
In a volcano's heart
Ominously glow red.

Rumbles and shaking,
Ground refinding a new
Resting spot.

Trials challenge
Even the most prepared,
Who work to use them.

Doughnuts have holes,
Space to contemplate
Their best part.

Split in half,
A meal, a workload, an atom,
Not your true Self.

Light finds a way to enter,
Like water
Running downhill.

They never forget us,
Even when we
Forget Them.

Spring is a crowd of tulips
Waving colors
At the surly sky.

Sirens moaning
In the distance,
Warning of life's brevity.

Love knits up the
Worn-out spots in life,
   With golden threads of light.

Cymbals crash,
Announcing the curtain drawn
   On a new horizon.

Our long time-body
Has twists and turns,
   But follows a straight line home.

Many factors
Comprise a pure heart,
But only one counts.

Saying goodbye,
When a role is ended,
Is a sad but heartfelt ritual.

All isn't lovely,
But, neutrally received,
All is acceptable.

A broken heart
Bleeds light,
    The very thing that mends it.

Hearty soup, made with love,
Reconstructs the scrambled
    Fabric of our health.

Holding together
Means more
    Than arm in arm.

Warriors for light courageously
Step into darkness,
Release weapons and shine.

Gracious and kind,
Our benefactors
Have infinite patience.

Step on a crack
But don't
Fall through one.

Even being upside down
We don't fall
Off the Earth.

From space
The Earth looks unpopulated;
Details matter.

There really is no illusion,
It's all here, now;
Missing – our fine attention.

Like clay
We are molded into
What They perceive is us.

Since our makers
Are invisible,
We falsely claim achievements.

Love every ounce
Of your life,
Good friends have left theirs.

Light surrounds us,
Even when the Sun hides.
    Time to see with different orbs.

Transitions from one phase to next:
Doorways, bridges, birthdays,
    Marriages; all describe us.

Running down the gravel drive
Kitten chases
    Mom and seven ducklings.

A large bouquet of roses
Emanates pink perfume
 Throughout the house.

Blue sky, white clouds,
Ultra-green grass;
 Vine flowers climb to the roof.

Most treasured chest,
Leaking light,
 Holds the best gift in the world.

My hands shaking
After a close call,
　　Energy with nowhere to go.

Reality appears
Unperturbed,
　　By my anxiety.

Each second
Contains the world,
　　Awaiting our arrival.

The best thing
That could have happened,
Is today, this moment.

A sharp stinging burn
Turns my palm red,
Very hot pot lid bit me.

Determined, creative, soft,
Flexible and very vulnerable,
Humans are incomprehensible.

Resistance is an obstacle
To entering
A new level of existence.

Hesitancy is expected
For transition
Into unknown territory.

Courage and fortitude
Are requirements
To take the next step.

Darkened landscape,
Silhouetted pines on black hill,
Watch giant moon rise behind.

Night flying bats
Squeak at enormous beacon,
Making shadows on roofs.

A child sees everything
With wondering eyes,
Full of curious innocence.

Grounded in Earth,
Educated in breath,
Released in spatial ether.

Death
Shows the limit
Of opportunities.

Each day is a present,
Open it with
Presence.

Loud noises
Startle senses,
    Awaken awareness.

Streaming to Earth,
Meteors burn with momentum;
    Gifts from a fiery world above.

Cracks in the ground,
Dangerous;
    Cracks in attitudes, useful.

Painful moments
Sans fear
Are short-lived.

Interpreting meaning
In events of the day,
Belongs to angelic beings.

Cassandra was not
Happy with
Her gift.

Ignorance may be bliss;
Expecting the unexpected
A high challenge.

Fate will out,
Regardless of preparation,
Better to submit and accept.

A crack in the wall:
Good for wall of obstinance,
Bad for wall of fortitude.

Sometimes the crash
And rumble, creating chaos,
Is a paper tiger.

An owl perched on a lamppost.
May be an omen,
If you allow it to be.

Icons and cyphers
Point to archetypes
Beyond sight.

At this level, view may be hazy;
Clear landscape opens
    Before third eye.

Tulips galore:
Fragrance, color, beauty
    Enhance living.

Life or death?
Simple question?
    Easier if you are not stubborn.

Let all the light in
To surround you;
Immerse your Self in light.

Creativity is eternally
Spontaneous,
And miraculous.

When we are long gone,
Nature remains.
Earth has its own fate.

Time is short
With a loved one.
　　Long, with misery.

Too much sun burns;
There cannot be too much
　　Uncreated light.

Glowing horizon
Heralds the coming
　　Dawn.

We cannot argue
With Cupid's arrow,
It pierces where it will.

Moths and bats
At the doorway,
Even they are attracted to light.

A pearl sits in the half-shell
Gleaming in moonlight,
Reflecting my longing gaze.

Damp and dreary,
My eyelids heavy,
This morning starts slowly.

Revelations happen,
Infrequently,
As if a light is switched on.

Drama is best kept on stage,
Moderate temper
Affords better outcomes.

Green velvet hills
Against bluest sky,
    Above foamy creek and wild iris.

Crystal pendant
Between the brows
    Has many invisible facets.

Red roses in the early sun,
Beauty before breakfast,
    A good omen.

Walk with me,
Double delight,
　　Double the light.

A sudden insight
Can shock,
　　And drive us sane.

Reality can abruptly appear
Outside of us,
　　Or inside of us.

Vibrations of lightning
Are loud and bright:
    A piercing scream from beyond.

Reality slices through
A simple moment
    With searing clarity.

Pink and yellow climbing roses,
In the backyard,
    Impart an exquisite fragrance.

Each day opens with Sun,
Drama unfolds,
Draws to a close with stars.

Actors on the stage,
Script is written,
But who gets to read it?

Reduced to blank inner world,
Spontaneous chance appears,
Ageless being peers out.

This side of the rainbow,
Colors are restricted to seven,
    On the other side lies freedom.

Light a candle
For each year of sharing
    Life on Earth.

As consciousness
Is not functions,
    Is a body actually necessary?

So much of life on Earth
Is about functions,
    The allurement is strong.

A whiff of your perfume
Is more than enough
    To thrill my senses.

Black and white,
Good for cats,
    Bad for attitudes.

Changes are aspects of life;
Revolutions, wars, chaos,
　　Are controlled by gods.

Stick a fork in it,
It's done
　　If it's tender.

We are tender,
And so very close
　　To being served upwards.

Angels depicted with swords
Are warriors for truth,
Protecting sacred states.

Book learning is essential,
Most valued is
What experience teaches us.

An ocean of stars,
Fed by the milky river,
Is home to many galaxies.

Solar flare,
Magnetic field alert,
   Gorgeous rosy sky.

Powerful music raging
Through senses,
   Reverberating echoes into dawn.

A squeak on the chalkboard
Can suffice to
   Upgrade a moment.

Cemeteries,
A good reminder
Of Time's ultimate end.

We are sensitive beings,
Our creativity enables culture,
But our minds can destroy it.

Living can cause stress,
So does the threat
Of not living.

Sometimes broken things
Release energy
    We didn't know we had.

Humor is often
Based on
    Flouted expectations.

Reverberations of a gong
Awaken the sluggish soul
    Who listens.

Friction is a gift;
Open slowly,
Don't panic.

Use perspective and relativity,
When absorbing
Disturbing shocks.

Frivolous behavior
Not as dangerous,
As wrong thinking.

Step carefully,
Left foot forward,
    Reside in both worlds.

The universe is vast
And mostly empty,
    Inner and outer space are alike.

When the inner voices start,
It is good to ask,
    Who's talking?

If the aim is correct,
The arrow
Will hit the target.

Just as the wind races
Across the bending grass,
The nimble adapt to change.

Light can be blocked
But never eliminated.
Holy light is uncreated.

Only love
Has the strength
   To relinquish the self.

Movement can encourage
An illusion
   Of reality.

On a dark road,
Shivers begin with
   The screech of an owl.

Eerie feelings,
Like watching eyes,
Make little hairs rise.

Day reveals harmless furniture,
Not enemies,
Hiding in dark shadows.

Seeing deeper
Into life
Reveals shallow waters.

Dancing with willow sprites,
Tiny fairies
Light rainbow lanterns.

Old forgotten myths
Cherished in childhood,
Leave trails of misty memory.

Deeper meaning
Can be derived
With third eye.

Splinters and shards
Shoot out from broken
Promises and lodge in tears.

Light is silent,
Quiet radiance
Surrounds the shadowless.

Invisible being shouting at me
With closed mouth:
"Be awake!"

Do we change,
Or do we become
More our Selves?

A flower can grow
Even through
A crack in a rock.

Lonely hearts
Call to each other
But seldom meet.

Hard times
Provide a lesson in
    Frugality.

Becoming smaller
Is a benefit
    Of learning humility.

To ascend,
Giving up everything,
    Doesn't mean only objects.

Storms occur
When contrasting forces
    Erupt together.

She turns her face from me;
Disappointment
    Is difficult for us both.

Nothing
Is much better
    Than it would seem.

In the quiet wake
Of thoughts,
    Profound silence opens.

Am I in the moment,
Or is the moment in me,
    Or are we the same thing?

People and times are bound
Together,
    A new age cannot divide them.

Outside time
There are no
    Moments.

Time and movement
Appear connected;
    Not so, speed of thought.

Who will I be
In the mystery of existence
    Without moments?

A crack in the wall
Of mechanicality
    Is a start.

Events develop as Fate wills,
Tiniest flaw allows
    Presence to change direction.

Not easy to be
A new person,
    But, O, so simple.

A mirror reflects your face.
What reflects
     Who you really are?

What is real in me
Meets
     What is real in you.

A vulture at my door,
Not a good
     Omen.

The earth smells green
For only a few more days,
    Scorching Summer advances.

Very hot sun burning eyes;
Shade, the only relief until
    Evening's cooling breezes.

Thunderbolt of truth
Hits the frozen wall of lies,
    And splits real from unreal.

To lighten the heavy burden
Add more
    Light.

Gods' gifts
At times seem harsh,
    Interrupting smooth sleep.

Friction is
Traction,
    If used properly.

The only way to
Change the future
Is to change the present.

Light fills all the cracks
In my being,
I am whole again.

Low flying helicopter,
Loud premonition of fire?
No, only safety survey.

Love is never truly lost,
Heart has been revamped
    To hold even more love.

Mountain lion in the backyard,
No time for omens,
    Just run.

In the eyes of my cat
That feline looked
    As big as a mountain.

To read omens,
Language from higher world
Must be learned.

In a fight
With Nature,
Nature wins.

When snakes come to visit,
Better to rethink welcoming
House guests.

King of the Mountain,
And King of snakes,
   Both in same surprising day.

More than light
Enters through
   Cracks.

Omens aren't really
Good or bad;
   Omens signal us to be awake.

Judgment is a plague
Affecting only humans,
    The animal world is immune.

The world is larger
Than our conception,
    We are more than we know.

Sister and brother
Contrast and complement
    The sacred Self.

Oppressive heat
Descends upon the foothills,
 Summer has a foot in the door.

Anguish and misery
Follow those
 Whom fate abandons.

Zeus in his mighty form
Sends electric bolts to Earth,
 Shocking eyes, ears, psyche.

When worlds interpenetrate,
Strange things
Can happen.

Priorities sharpen,
Trivialities disappear,
We know who and where we are.

Stay in your body,
Don't wander,
Home is your starting place.

The golden moment is perfect,
And not perturbed
By our reactions to it.

Openings between worlds
Are rare and small,
Leave all behind.

Spring strives to grow
Everything it can,
Summer burns it brown.

Symbols are only pointers;
We make the choice
    To enter the present moment.

The biggest shock
Separating worlds
    Is Death.

Truth can be managed,
Reality may be hard to take
    In one gulp.

Planets move against
Stationary starry background,
Illusion of perception.

The magician waves his wand,
The world disappears,
Replaced by nothing.

Screeching brakes,
Small hairs rise up –
Where's kitty?

When the real
Penetrates the unreal,
Splintering shards sting.

Truth to illusion
Is as
Day to night.

Questions arise,
Are we ready
For the answers?

All we have is
Tomorrow,
But only if we have today.

Predictions are wily,
Like the weather,
Hard to pin down.

Tilt your head,
Look up,
The sky alive with light.

Having your way
Isn't always good,
Be careful what you wish for.

The opportunities
To be had
Are always in the present.

If it feels like you are
Losing your mind,
Rejoice!

The blown
Mind boundary
Opens to a great expanse.

Moderation and patience:
Virtues leading to
Wisdom.

Extremes and absolutes:
Excesses leading to
Imbalance.

The flags are out,
Every tree is waving leaves,
　　Summer Solstice is here.

Sharp edges separate
Each of us
　　From everything else.

Imperfections
Do not exist
　　In ultimate truth.

Infinite variety
Of natural Earth
    Is playful and dangerous.

Gradual changes soothe,
Abrupt changes
    Shock.

As personality
Falls away,
    Who is left?

Hardly any
Nighttime left,
    Sun reigns supreme.

The ceiling of our world,
Painted black and blue,
    Would be cruel without stars.

When senses are attentive,
A sudden loud crash
    Reverberates strongly.

Omens portend
Approaching ominous
And eye-opening ordeals.

When new light
Enters the scene,
Things look quite different.

Future sends shockwaves
Forward and backward
Into the present.

To know your fate,
Become
    The Self.

An omen of
Impending death,
    Implies role completion.

Don't refuse the cup
When offered;
    Gracefully transition.

Omens, like beauty,
Belong to beholders;
Hold on to Be.

Clean, strong and elegant,
Stride forth
With a light heart.

Old fears and worries
Fade in the clear light
Of pure nothingness.

The dance is short,
The music stops,
The curtain closes.

Endings are good.
They make room
For beginnings.

We love and are grateful
To the extent
Of our capacity.

Emotional strength
Develops via
    Transformed suffering.

The body reacts
To harsh shocks,
    The Self does not waver.

Interpreting signals
From the starry world,
    Begs a cosmic language.

We can't always go right,
Or we would be back
    Where we started.

The crescent moon
Hides her face,
    But smiles at my foibles.

The writing is on the wall.
Reading and knowing it
    Will not replace living it.

Macbeth received truth;
It did not prevent
His play.

Preaching truth
Will not thaw
Frozen ears.

A crack appearing
In cemented opinion
Portends new attitude.

Heartbeat, breath,
Day, night;
Rhythms define living.

Messages are sent,
Slicing through our day.
Do we receive them?

When the heart speaks
Its truth,
Lies and fears fall away.

Hold close
Those who value
Highest light.

Worlds in worlds,
A Chinese box
Of conundrum.

Unraveling this mystery
Is a lifetime
Of piercing each moment.

Zeus struck his staff
Into Earth,
  Reverberating around the world.

A ringing gong
Is a loud and deep sound
  Challenging our sleep.

Six tiny quail
Follow their mother
  Into the blackberry bush.

Dark heavy clouds
Create deep shadows
On the growing rice paddy.

Listen for the soundless
Music emanating
From the stars.

Star melody
Courses through
Daylight and bodies.

When there is knocking
At the door,
　　Open with gracious welcoming.

Connectedness of events
May be discerned by internal
　　Review and realization.

A backward look
Over current decisions
　　May help discern options.

Nothing is ever truly lost,
Except that
Which was never real.

Lower energies ascend
When least expected,
While drifting.

A gunshot!
Birds fly up wildly,
Kitty runs home.

Wildfire season:
Brush gets a haircut,
    Neighbors rethink grounds.

Craters and canyons
Hold secret caves,
    Dark hidden dwellings.

Night creatures
Are not so scary
    In Dawn's reveal.

Air tankers overhead,
Ominous sign
Of fire evacuation.

Good and bad
Are properties
Of unreality.

Dragging your feet
Won't change results,
Just make you tardy.

Step on a crack
But don't
Fall through.

Ophelia slept
In a watery bed of flowers;
Rest is restorative, not final.

Smoke visible from afar;
Alarming in strong wind,
Headed this way.

A flash of brightest light
Making eyelids squint,
    Could open invisible eye.

Halfway through the year,
Flags waving high,
    Dangerous fireworks coming.

Cracks can be repaired;
Take care,
    Shattering more difficult.

Peer through
The crack in the door;
　　Watch your nose isn't clipped.

Shocks may be pleasant
Or unpleasant,
　　Accomplishing change of state.

Sleep-filled eyes
Are forced open
　　In brilliant light of crisis.

The gods beat their drums,
Summoning angels
With flapping wings of light.

Bow down
To receive
Offerings from on high.

Do not dwell on past sleep,
Presence in this moment
Is the only shelter.

Amazing light penetrates
To core existence,
  Brightening shadowed lives.

Care for each subject
Of attention,
  Lest heart starvation ensues.

Reality is only harsh
To that which
  Does not actually exist.

Wolf shocks kitty
Into being roof bound,
   Wild animals are afoot.

Magic attracts us,
A world of miracles
   Pleases imagination.

Interruption implies
Momentum;
   Each moment merits attention.

Easy to predict
The flower
From such lovely buds.

Slide from quicksand of guilt
Into pit of despair;
Don't go near it.

Decisions and consequences
Make up our lives,
But only horizontally.

A vertical life
Is dictated
By higher powers.

Knotted scowling clouds
Threaten storm,
Then recede in high flight.

To see far – get up high;
To see more,
Be more.

To grow wings,
Sprout nubs,
Practice letting go.

A glass of wine,
The glow in your eyes,
My heart swells with love.

Without preparation,
It is foolish
To attempt flight without wings.

Great being is admired
In art, sports, business;
    Being in presence is invisible.

Tear off the bandage
All at once,
    Small sacrifice for culmination.

Blue-gray dawn creeps over
Mountain top,
    Bleeds rays in all directions.

Inky dark climbs
The trellis,
    Each evening of my life.

The architecture
Of reality,
    Is beyond description.

Try to not complain;
A symptom
    Of lacking gratitude.

We are rattled and shaken
At their discretion;
　　Our job to use it.

Be as kind to yourself
As to others,
　　Kindness evinces respect.

Illness or injury
May modify actions,
　　Let nothing impede presence.

The fiery Summer
Snarls her way
Through the burned grasses.

The phone rings,
A knock at the door,
Be where you are, regardless.

Broken glass under my foot,
Wear shoes,
Sweep floor.

Protection becomes a prison,
Seed must crack open
    For a plant to grow.

Brush is cut,
Yard is swept,
    Stage is set.

A loud crack
Stops all thought,
    Raises hackles and states.

Defenses are low
When asleep;
Solution: wake up.

A shooting star
Aimed at the heart of Mars
Threatens endless war.

When the spirits of air collide
With the mountains of Earth,
Thunder is born.

Otherworldly communications,
Though difficult to decipher,
Still affect higher mind.

Our lives revolve around
Our personal fate,
We stretch to help each other.

Omens abound
When angels
Are present.

"Ominous" and "Omens"
Have a lot
In common.

To be startled awake
Can create fear,
Or a sense of true reality.

Take heart,
Climb high,
Don't look down.

When an omen
Proves true,
    Surprise is a lack of faith.

Keep your head up,
Shoulders back,
    Eyes forward.

Those triggers
That set you off,
    Let them lie fallow.

Extremely heated air
Madly circulates
In more than my oven.

Take aim,
Be firm,
Follow through.

Familiarity feels safe,
An illusion
Fostered by bodily comfort.

Laurel leaves crown
The dome of triumph,
    Invisible success accomplished.

We are so lucky
To share the success
    Of gods.

Perfect silence
Is a gift
    Rarely attained.

The stark vision
Of sleeping humanity
Unveils ultimate consequence.

Trials and tribulations
Await a troubled heart;
Submit in silence.

July, a month of
Work and fiery heat,
Heralded by fireworks.

Calliope, Muse of Poetry,
Laid down her quill
And listened for deep silence.

Slow changes
Are usurped by
Sudden transformations.

Water may cool slowly,
But becomes ice
All in a moment.

Lovers leave behind
Woes and worries,
    To rush into each other's arms.

Patterns swim before our eyes,
Breaking up and reassembling,
    Deeper meaning elusive.

Reading the cues,
A tricky business,
    Prophecy best left to mystics.

Catastrophe can
Break the dam
On sleepy illusions.

From horizon to horizon
Spectacular reality
Shimmers into view.

The balance of yin and yang
Are an inseparable unit,
Remember Winter in Summer.

Empty your quiver
Into target's center,
    Aim with conscious attention.

Ringing bells announce
Union of sweetest maid
    With stalwart son.

Lay rushes on the path,
Raise the flowered garlands;
    Honored guest approaching.

Alarming sirens
Wail through steamy dusk;
　　Emergency aid to the rescue.

Dive in,
The water's fine;
　　Immerse in liquid silk.

Runes and glyphs
Adorn rocks and walls,
　　Transmitting past messages.

Molten rock river
Flows down mountainside
    And sizzles into steaming sea.

A closed fist
Cannot suffice like
    An open hand.

If you know too much,
It is scary
    To live.

Shock waves reverberate
Around the world,
    Creating new patterns.

The darkest cave
Cannot block
    The undiminished light.

Our Sun's plasma
Affects our magnetic field
    By firing intermittent charges.

Without cosmic input
We would wither
    And shrivel into coal.

Our heated blood
And cooling skin
    Encase a wordless miracle.

The startling reality
Is that we have always
    Been in exactly the right place.

Braid your hair,
Polish your shoes,
    Dress to receive high visitant.

Voice of high lord
Resonates through
    Dense bodies like lightning.

Owl lands atop the pillar;
Is Athena guiding
    Ultimate end of this play?

The challenge
Is to be grateful
For the prickly path upwards.

Songs of lust and passion
Rage across the stage to
Clash in open air.

Signs were there
For all to read,
Blindness cushioned reality.

Omens abide eons,
Decipher markings
In deep mountain caves.

To see farther,
Turn on
The light.

The miracle of existence
Can be taken for granted
At our peril.

The span between
Birth and death,
Is soul incubation.

True birth
Will reveal
Real parents.

Open the gift
On your day of birth,
Of immortality.

Until that day
Watch the cues,
  Earn your wings.

Estranged from
Your true self,
  Go back to basics.

Remember to be grateful,
Reprioritize necessities,
  Open heart, close mouth.

Fate's hurtled spears
Sometimes land in your life,
Accept and be grateful.

Survey the landscape
Of burning embers,
Nature gone awry.

No one has to teach my cat
We are always here;
But recognition isn't automatic.

It takes death
To learn
We are not the body.

Generous, kind, and reliable;
Qualities of high-minded being,
Admired but hard acquired.

Who moves your hand?
Who has your thoughts?
Who sees through your eyes?

High flying hawk
Dives low,
    Unlucky field mouse.

One moment
Is all it takes
    For a drastic change.

The setting sun
Reflected in your eyes
    Fills me with longing.

Splitting the atom
Wasn't nearly as stunning
As uncreated light.

The ground shakes
And rolls over,
Grumpy in its sleep.

When the soul
Knows true home,
All is said and done.

Growing wings
May be hard work,
   But invaluable.

Wild and free spirit
Knows no bondage,
   Attracted to brilliant light.

Clear essence awareness
Of Self in present moment
   Connects with vertical levels.

Separation from false identity
Is work of a lifetime or more,
    Each present moment counts.

Shortcuts occur at the
Discretion of
    Angels.

Superior light
Of self-realized beings
    Is here with us in the present.

The future sprouts from
Seeds planted in the past,
    Nurtured in the present.

Omens are signs
Posted in eternity,
    Visible here.

Why bother
With what does not
    Truly exist?

Inner peace
Is born
Of deep silence.

Fate may twist and turn,
But brooks
No argument.

Tomorrow's light
Will not lighten today's
Shadows.

Avoiding change
Will only delay
Inevitable.

Take heart,
Nothing is as bad
As fear portrays it.

Short trip,
Change of scene,
New possibilities.

Eclipse of our star
Caused havoc in the past;
Now, thousands flock to it.

A flexible mind stretches;
A brittle one snaps apart,
Madness awaits.

Chaos is curbed
By organization
Externally and internally.

A dark heart
Craves light
Even unknowingly.

Misfortune befalls
Everyone at times,
Staying even, necessary.

Beautiful Pacific,
White-crested ocean,
Cool and inviting.

Change of environment
Helpful to spot
Habits and patterns.

Lavender fragrance,
Purplely sweet,
Fills senses with calm.

Unexpected events
Can stimulate
Or shatter consciousness.

The clang of metal
Striking stone
    Jangles ears and nerves.

Holding a newborn
Challenges
    Preconceived notions of age.

Seemingly never-ending
Chain of experiences
    Is our life.

Break through
To a new level,
　　Leave old self behind.

The light that is us
Starts from a god shard
　　Awarded at birth.

The growth of being
Depends upon right attitudes
　　And a willingness to yield.

Cry tomorrow,
Swing wide the opening
　　To love and joy, today.

Cracks appear
When the first point of light
　　Escapes bonds.

The real
Is seldom troubled
　　By the unreal.

To step from the darkness
Into the light,
　　Open inner eye.

Making the right connections
And keeping them,
　　Allows the way to open.

To make the right
Connections,
　　Start by being grateful.

Being happy is a choice,
Not dependent
    Upon circumstances.

Look deeper
Into the world.
    Surface can be misleading.

Being is earned
By suffering
    The unknowable.

To unravel the enigma,
Use the method
Of no thought.

In the quest
For immortality,
Lose your wits.

To look different, change hair;
To feel different,
Change patterns.

Flowers at the door,
Beautiful invitation
To enter.

She walks in silence
Through brightest light,
Hair shining golden.

Though I can't see your face,
You are near,
Waiting for me to find you.

A natural spring
Sends cool water into air,
    Refreshes throats and moods.

The intangible spirit
Is beyond destruction,
    Outside corruption.

The human soul is vulnerable,
Needs education, nurturing
    And outside help to evolve.

Put thinking aside,
Look deep into your heart,
Surrender to Love.

Clarity comes
As illusions
Are burned away.

The meaning in words
Comes through,
When the medium is prepared.

Between us
And the light
Is only an illusionary barrier.

Pure white light –
Perfect, clear and strong –
Begins and ends Earth play.

Plants struggle to reach
Nurturing Sun,
Living things consume light.

To be who you are
In your life,
Is a relief and a joy.

A funeral isn't somber,
Only serious,
Respecting those who suffer.

Sun-warmed peaches
Bend boughs,
Waiting for a pie surround.

The shock of presence
Resonates through the soul
Into higher realms.

We are generously given
Our best thoughts,
No place for vanity.

When we believe
Only what we see,
Illusion is reinforced.

It is unfortunate
That seeing
Is believing.

That which is invisible
Is more real
Than images before our eyes.

To see beauty,
It must be recognized
By residing beauty.

Vision is a great aid
And a great deceiver;
To see more, open third eye.

Ecstatic creative freedom
Couples with
Awareness of awareness.

Love marries
Joy
Via discipline.

Startling shocks,
Scary moments,
Provide refocusing opportunity.

Shared present awareness
Increases potential,
For exponential development.

Free play
Is essential
For growth of soul.

Beauty of youth
Lives inside
    Aged crusty exterior.

Joy rises up
Spilling into light,
    Remembering you.

Trees grew
Without talking
    About growing.

The force of water
Quickens growth
Of the natural world.

No amount of darkness
Can quell
The indomitable light.

Inner light
Is greater
Than exterior brightness.

The space field
Holds the world together,
   Just as love binds lovers.

One candle glows,
But a hundred
   Make a blaze.

Particles of light
Ride undulating waves
   Directly through eye pupil.

As cold is lack of heat,
So is dark lack of light,
        Both are nothing in themselves.

        Some things
Are more real
        Than others.

        Well rounded
Means equal growth
        In all inner spheres.

When there are
No more words,
   Listen for the music.

Listening is
More important
   Than hearing.

In silence
Listening makes
   Ears open wider.

The signs were there,
But the language was vague,
    It could only be read by heart.

Gentle souls,
Cast aside your heavy cloaks,
    Join the innocent choir.

An archer is poised
To release his arrow,
    At a precise moment in time.

Timing is essential
In every
Event.

Love sharpens his arrows,
In anticipation
Of Earth's beauty.

Summer's heat
Makes roast pigeons
Without an oven.

The only quest
Worth the venture
Is an internal trek.

Our source
Is inner
Light.

We are supported
In ways beyond
Our ability to perceive.

With maturity of soul
Comes understanding
And gratitude.

A child peers out
From ancient eyes,
And knows joy.

Seeds of the future
Can be recognized,
Even before sprouting.

If God is no thing,
Nothing must be wonderful,
Simpler the better.

Pointers to God
Must be space itself,
Closest to nothing.

If up is better than down,
No wonder
We so want to fly.

A small sacrifice
Can feel large,
    Like the tongue in your mouth.

Life streams like a river,
Suddenly,
    There's an eyeopener.

Trees, lungs of Earth,
Exhale,
    So we can inhale.

Technical fantasy
May have blunted
Awe of the miraculous.

Our existence
Is a miracle,
Moment by moment.

Deer are thirsty,
Rain
Is only a memory.

Champagne bubbles
Rise,
To the occasion.

Fire is essential and lifegiving,
But combustible air
And tinderbox ground is scary.

The garden of Earth
Is slowly becoming
A human ant hill.

To look beyond
The obvious,
    Is to become subtle.

The quiet place
At the self's center,
    Passes final barrier.

A four-alarm fire
Penetrates all levels,
    Provoking immediate response.

Water travels around the Earth,
No passport or boundaries
Inhibit its intrepid journey.

Coming to rest internally
Is a good starting place
To review our blessings.

Being open to change
Is a strength,
As change is continuous.

Spherical is a perfect shape:
Stars, Earth, bubbles, eyes,
Perhaps even our souls.

Friendship promotes
Goodwill toward everyone,
Positive bonds influence all.

Golden ring,
Symbol of deep connection,
Encircles the heart finger.

A large fire north of us
Is sending its smoke
   Ominously our way.

Last day of July
Fading with the light;
   Relaxing reflection time.

August is upon us;
Final gasps of heat,
   Promises of cooler evenings.

There is a world we share,
And a world of our own,
Which we guard carefully.

All worlds
Not based in reality
Are illusory.

They hear our prayers,
All our requests aren't satisfied,
For our benefit.

When a hard shell
Breaks open,
    A baby chick peeps forward.

Gestation needs
Protection,
    Until it doesn't.

The shell of our bodies
Will eventually break:
    What will peep forward?

Holding forth
On opinions,
        Isn't worth the air expenditure.

Nimbus of pure light
Surrounds the head
        Of the beloved.

Love nourishes our
Very bones,
        We would perish without love.

The freedom to be
True to ourselves,
Is always here.

While Europe holidays,
We enjoy visitors
From around the world.

To be grateful
Is a higher state of
Realization.

Finer energies
Are deployed
To see truth.

In a moment,
Events can lead us
In a new direction.

Inner stillness
Maintains our true direction,
Regardless of circumstances.

The timeless aspect
Of eternity,
Is difficult for linear thinking.

The steward of the household
Keeps order,
Outside is wild divine chaos.

Omens of good luck,
Can feel fortunate;
Attention from gods enigmatic.

Vignettes of etched moments
Survive within each of us;
Presence fuels memory.

Cast away fears and desires;
Be happy to breathe,
All that is truly yours remains.

Clouds obscuring Sun's face,
Threatening rain,
Offering brief respite from heat.

Small white cup of water,
Secured in two hands
    Is proffered to the supplicant.

Meteor shower,
Super moon, planet sightings,
    August delights afoot.

One shining water droplet
Clinging to a rose petal,
    Reflects the world inverted.

We cannot pray enough
At the altar of Love,
There is no replacement.

Knowing oneself
Is not about identity,
But about field of awareness.

We are higher centers,
We are Light,
We are awareness of both.

Small identity
Is lost,
In the sea of Knowingness.

Knowing, we are strong,
Humble, grateful,
Uniquely our Selves.

Contradictions exist
For the small self
Seeking identity.

If memory is lost
Do we disappear?
We are not memory.

If we change our name
Are we someone else?
We are not our names.

Who we are
Is a channel into awareness,
Knowing itself.

To be God's spies,
We must tap into
    Rarified field of awareness.

We lose our self
By being
    Our Self.

The body is an anchor
Until we are ready
    To peruse the stars.

Astro philosophers
Live their study,
    Moment by moment.

To enjoy full realization,
Empty your cup
    Of all preconceived.

Live as a child,
Always seeing
    Anew.

Through this entity I call myself,
Energy evolves from god
To God.

A rainbow
Is the beauty
Of the spectrum of light.

Angels mirror
The love they have received,
By serving.

Go unshod into the river
Of awareness;
    Relax resistance, surrender.

History repeats itself.
To predict the future,
    Review the past.

Although result is unforeseen,
Faith is presence
    In this moment.

Love, presence,
Realized awareness,
Are all one field of energy.

The exquisite movements
Of high ballet
Tell a story all can understand.

Omens can point the way,
Even when sealed Fate
Opens to the elements.

Pandora looked where
She shouldn't,
    Woes and miseries escaped.

Eve tasted forbidden fruit,
Lot's wife looked back,
    Queens cannot resist mischief.

Cassandra was cursed|
With warnings
    No one wanted.

Truth isn't always pleasant;
Light and realization
Are above pleasure and pain.

After years observing Si-Dos,
It is a joy to understand
The perfection of existence.

There is time enough,
In Eternity,
For everything to manifest.

Go with eyes and heart
Wide open,
Love leads the way.

We are grateful
For our spiritual education,
Mostly wordless.

To find true home,
Stop looking,
Start being there.

There is so much history
In Europe
    Depicted in stone and paint.

Humans have ruined
Much of Earth's beauty,
    But also added to it as well.

Don't give up;
When you are already there,
    Realization comes when it will.

A river cannot be a mirror.
To see your face
    Water must be still.

Springs gush water forth
Right through cracks in rocks,
    Anxious to feed creeks and rivers.

To steer your boat
Through the river of love,
    Let light fill your sails.

The natural world
Must have found us alien,
　　Before the stars sang welcome.

Were omens
Sent to the dinosaurs
　　About the meteor?

Grace in movement
Pleases the eye,
　　Conveys love through motion.

Electrons crash, cars crash,
But when galaxies crash,
    It's a much different scale.

Wipe your eyes,
Start again,
    Each attempt you get closer.

Three cheers for the stars
Lighting the way
    For travelers during new moon.

Even the darkest night
Knows coming light
Will dispel all doubts.

Let this missive
Be an omen of love
Coming to you.